THE GLIMMER

Shazea Quraishi is a Pakistani-born Canadian poet and translator based in London. A selection of her work was included in the Bloodaxe/Complete Works anthology *Ten: new poets from Spread the Word* in 2010, and her first pamphlet, *The Courtesans Reply*, was published by flipped eye in 2012. *The Art of Scratching*, her first book-length collection, was published by Bloodaxe Books in 2015. Her second book of poetry, *The Glimmer*, was published by Bloodaxe in 2022. She received a Brooklease Grant from the Royal Society of Literature in 2015 and an award from the Artists International Development Fund of the British Council and Arts Council England in the same year.

SHAZEA QURAISHI

THE GLIMMER

BLOODAXE BOOKS

ISBN: 978 1 78037 633 2

First published 2022 by
Bloodaxe Books Ltd,
Eastburn,
South Park,
Hexham,
Northumberland NE46 1BS

www.bloodaxebooks.com
For further information about Bloodaxe titles
please visit our website and join our mailing list
or write to the above address for a catalogue.

Supported using public funding by
ARTS COUNCIL
ENGLAND

Cover design: Neil Astley & Pamela Robertson-Pearce.

Printed in Great Britain by Bell & Bain Limited, Glasgow, Scotland, on
acid-free paper sourced from mills with FSC chain of custody certification.

CONTENTS

THE GLIMMER

DAY 1

She wakes to birdsong   sun slats on the floor
suitcase by the door spills clothes   quiet
of the house a cocoon   a skin

At the table she waits for the mouse to thaw
    scalpel   tweezers   calipers
    pins   pipecleaners   wire   scissors
    needle   thread   straw
Begins
taking apart
putting together

A white mouse, a feeder mouse

soft drift of white
his modest truth disarms me

forehead
ears   feet
        mouth
        a dim rose
        with teeth

I admire this
raw meat of us
this ease

DAY 2

Sunrise
the highest tree in the garden is first to be lit
Birds come   one red-bellied   another bright yellow
black-headed   black wings tipped with white
another   a pair

Sky blue as the bucket by the tap
air cool   an ant crosses her foot
bees in the lavender bush

   A mother and her small son hurry past the gate
   schoolbag in her hand

A bird perches in a leafless tree
dun-coloured   long-tailed   quiet
watches her watching
preens under its wings

   The mother returns
   releasing her hair from its band

Her hands   intent   precise   thinking
    miracle how living works   stops
    careful labour to preserve restore   what?
    ~~limbo?~~
    past-in-present perhaps   an imprint   a 3-dimensional
    holding   ~~of memory~~   of once-being

She once heard someone say this is craft it lacks edge
    (advantage power urgency force)
gets up to shift thoughts

From the blue house next door   song
a voice testing lines   as a tightrope walker
tests for tension   before stepping out onto the wire
strung between 2 stopping places

My beloved is weather, she is cloud, rainshower,
a day dawning generous, bright with birds.

Streets freshly watered, a telephone line
is strung as if pearled, with white after white after white bird...

Sound of a phone ringing

She remembers
swimming in a river by her brother's house
the current cold   insistent
How once she let it carry her too far before climbing the high bank
to walk back over pine needles   hard earth   stones
How he watched from a window
until he saw her
red swimsuit flickering through the trees

A white mouse (2)

what has a white mouse to show us

I meet him
white   mute   item

    (fate
    air hums with it)

he was
he is

    I sew him shut
    wish him home

DAY 3

Morning
suggestion of heat

At the river
she undresses on the grassy bank   slips
into the thrilled water   oh
   to be here
air water world against skin
everywhere   green   blue
living things living

Walking back   she meets the painter of miniatures
his colouring   planes of his face   neat beard
remind her of her brother
feel   like home

We made our own brushes
with squirrel hair.
Our teacher used to say
'with bad weapons
you cannot fight'.

Lahore is a city
of gardens, so
there are many squirrels.
You go with apples and
they come. Also
the gardeners know you so
when a squirrel
dies, they bring it.

First take the straw of a
pigeon feather. Clean it.
Take squirrel hair
and pass it through the hole.
Clean bamboo for the stick,
tie it with thread.
That's the qalam.

There was a strict discipline –
leaving shoes outside the studio
sitting cross-legged on the floor
for hours on end holding your
breath while painting – as if there was
a defined outline and we had
to accept the challenge of
staying within its confines.

DAY 4

Morning light   coffee
white butterfly on the coral bougainvillea
   The average lifespan of a butterfly is a month   this small
   butterfly will live perhaps a week
   that's a full life

Hummingbird?
perhaps the idea of the bird
   something
      speed and stop
         says hummingbird

Yesika   the woman at the shop   said if you wait for it
or want it too much   it won't come
   How to not want something?

Jingle from the gas truck
announces its arrival at the crossroads

A white mouse (3)

hiatus
time teems   thaws

she ate
she saw

    oh muse   most
    whose tame wish
    was oats

(how I adore this somewhat wise housemate)

Night   grass needles her skin
body blanketed by stars

Sudden light on the terrace of the red house next door
2 dancers emerge   the woman like a sleepwalker moves
    sheer red dress
    long legs shine through
the man follows   with his eyes   dark linen suit
abruptly she stops
topples   like a tree   he catches her
again
again

My beloved is weather, she is cloud, rainshower,
a day dawning generous, bright with birds.

Rain is beginning, and rain is ending,
longed-for and sudden, as heavy, as light as birds.

Beauty's a gift, and beauty's a cage,
a thunder of wingbeats, a day and a night of birds.

Streets freshly watered, a telephone line
is strung as if pearled, with white after white after white bird.

The breeze brings a name woven with flowers,
bestows on the trees a blessing, a first light of birds.

Come to the river, to its bed full of stones,
come rest on the green of its bank, a delight for birds.

What's in a name? Ava means voice,
melody, song... And song is the birthright of birds.

DAY 5

Dawn chorus
She takes the hummingbird from the freezer
The boy down the road found it under a hibiscus bush
they like red flowers
Chuparrosa   he called it   Rose-drinker
   Sometimes they sleep so deeply   *letargo*
   it's like they're dead   but this is not sleep   he said
   I checked

Nestled in the palm of her hand   wings tucked in as though cold
she regrets her wish to see one so close

Rose drinker

rise
keen siren

reside in rosier din

seek red
drink

On the radio   a local station
talk shifts between languages
each with its own soundscape
tonal music

Ultimately, as an artist
you're accountable to yourself.
Yeah, critics review
yeah, gatekeepers say
whether they want to do your play
or not; audiences clap or boo...
Ultimately, you
have to look at yourself and say
  Have I done the thing
  I set out to do?

For me the artistic enterprise is
I'm going to tell you
a story, a narrative that has been
shaped. If I was writing my actual life
story, I'd condense
that entire marriage in a footnote.

I wanted to look for inspirations,
things that were happening to me and project
them onto a fictional couple. My
constraint was motherhood.

Art is born of necessity.
I need to do this to sustain
myself, to maintain myself
or my sense of sanity
or whatever you call it.

Spiny pocket mouse

minute moppet
   eyes inky moons
   toe tips pink

tiny stoic
        once nosy   scooty

    untie time's knot
    postpone emptiness

Without you here, without your voice, yesterday was lost.
I move through hours, it's no use, today is lost.

If life's a stage, the theatre's dark; the actors left,
lines forgotten, set abandoned, playscript lost.

All night I wrote to you, awoke to find the pages gone,
the words that could have saved us, irrevocably lost.

Through the open window, a leaf, green as hope,
almost enters. A rush of wind, it drifts away, lost.

My beloved, in an armchair, drifts, elsewhere.
What to do but watch, and hope – believe – love outweighs loss.

DAY 8

She works   painstakingly removing pin feathers
    a memory
her brother tying flies   fish hook in a vice   tongue tip between
lips
silk   feather   his precise fingers

She takes his book from the shelf

> *The fan-wing   wide upright wings   curve outward*
> *well tied   a very beautiful fly*
> *The spent-wing represents the fly exhausted after its breeding flight*
> *more sparsely hackled   will settle farther into the surface film of*
> *the water   like a dead or dying creature*

Scott's oriole

stir
   cool stoic

cross isles
crest cities
roost

      resist soil's cloister

The boy   his name is Havi   returns with 4 hummingbirds
pitiful things   poorly preserved   bought from a man in the city
    They make powerful love-charms   he says   the bird with
    a keepsake from the beloved   covered with honey in a jar
    sealed with a spell

She tries to explain
    only animals who died a natural or unpreventable death...
sees his face
    thank you   she says quickly   and
    sadness has its own beauty

He is wearing the same blue t-shirt   freshly laundered
shy looks towards the animals on the shelf
She shows him the mouse curled up in a pale green china cup
fur so soft

    For you

When he is gone she examines the birds
one is smaller than any she's seen
    impossible wonder magic of it
    head the size of her fingernail
In her palm it weighs perhaps a penny
    iridescent throat feathers electric pink purple
    fat little body
Rot is beginning   nothing can be done except learn its name
    Bumblebee Hummingbird (*Atthis heloisa*)
that it lives in the Sierra Gorda   far from here

Despair pity anger in her throat
she makes a small pyre outside the back door
kindling   dried flowers   bed of stones
acrid smoke as it burns

Later she will lay the 3 remaining birds   side by side
on a bed of straw
in a box painted with red flowers

Word spreads
her freezer begins to fill

Volcano rabbit

torn bobtail
no antic

    coat
        tail
            rib

    coral ribbon   alit

vacant aria
a volt into air

The painter comes to tea
shy   the tiled kitchen shines
tea on the stove in a pink enamel pot
ginger   cardamom   sugar   milk

    People look at my work   think it's about death
    really it's about life   the fullness
    within time's holding of it

He dunks a biscuit in his tea
   pleasure she feels
sunlight streams through the window

In the corner   the neighbour's small black dog stirs
whimpers in his sleep
dirty black fur   low slung body   long ears   sweet trusting face
he likes the cool tiles

    Uncomfortable sometimes   stroking him   knowing
    what's under the fur   how things are put together
    how fragile we all are

When we apply paint,
it's so alive, it's
moving. When it dries,
it becomes dead.

I want to experience
the life of this medium
before it becomes
part of the work.

When we apply gold leaf
we turn off the fans.
In a film, I let it fly
*   it's like it's alive.*

They are always asking me
'as a Muslim artist…' and
'do you believe in Islam?'

Just look at my work
and talk about that.

DAY 13

Someone brings her   what is it?
   Ugly   not often she thinks this
Is it the pointy shrewish snout
dark bulging eyes long fingers toes bulbous tips
   what to do with it?

That night she dreams she is fluid
moving through water   light ripple-glimmers
across the blue tiled floor   she surfaces
    Huitzilopochtli the hummingbird god appears
    floating in the air   speaks
    words like wind through a door.

Mexican mouse opossum

supine campesino
no nip no pounce no noise
                    suspense

someone's cousin
                compassion comes

I coax   ~~escape?~~   ~~séance?~~
a sepia pause
immense comma

DAY 15

A dancer comes to her door
curly black hair   sweet smile
   Come to lunch?

Long table in the shade   embroidered tablecloths
flowers   figures   birds
Talk flows down the table
   Here is life   fully
A man gestures   white hair
lit from within
A tall dancer in a blue dress laughs   silk ripples
over her body   blonde hair cascades down her back
every movement   dance
   she tries not to stare

At Francis Bacon at the Tate,
I got this awful feeling I
was looking at a real artist.
I felt... not fraudulent, but
I started to think my art just
didn't stand up. I remember
feeling almost breathless. I think
I didn't paint for about two
weeks, because I felt like a sham.
It took me two weeks to think, Jack
that's Francis Bacon.
That's what he *did.*
This is what you *do*

You do ask yourself
Why am I here? What is my purpose?
It goes on and on, the questioning.

You're trying to stay alive,
you're trying to take pictures.

> *These are the consequences of*
> *your political decisions.*
> *Look, these are the consequences*
> *of your carelessness.*

I try to stay calm.
I try not to indulge myself
in this picture-taking.
It's something I was meant to do.

I never write 'about'
but 'from'.
This is the experience
of living in Palestine –
it shapes relationship
with language –
there's a lot of deletion,
there's a lot of negation.

Language reveals itself
within the silence of writing.
I've been struggling with this –
how can you write silence?

Many sufferings stem
from human thinking.
We are what we think.
Cinema can change thought.

I think life is void –
everyone fills it in their own way.
I do it with cinema.
This is the only amusing doll
remaining for me from my childhood.

Food is brought to the table
    jugs of cucumber water   hibiscus water
    salads   nopal cactus   avocado   tomato
    charred corn   cheese   salsa   tortillas   mezcal

New in the company I didn't yet grasp
how Pina worked, and she didn't explain.
I was lost until I realised
I had to pull myself up by my hair.

I saw her do Café Müller so often
I wanted to sense what she was feeling.
She moved as if she had a hole in her
belly, as if risen from the dead.

When Pina asked me to dance her part
I said yes. But I never learned it.
I wanted her to dance forever.

*She was so beautiful to watch when she
was watching us. In rehearsals I'd see her
sitting behind that desk, living every
moment with her dancers, full of all
the feelings we were having.*

*Pina watched me for 22 years
and that was longer than my parents.*

Talk turns to water   the river nearby
Christiana leads her behind the house
a pool   blue with sky
Parting the hedge   a gap   her house on the other side
　come anytime
　we sleep late

First light   birdsong
through the hedge   the pool
    oh   this
body of water   skin muscle bone breath
moving working wonder of it

    her shadow vague on the blue tiles below
    could be any thing creature cloud

above her the water ripples   stills
under water she flows
like thought passing
or sadness

Great-tailed grackle

late great talker
dark-attired glider
   aerial dagger

call   a creak   a clatter
a tilted tirade

altar   a cradle aglitter

      radiate elegiac grace

DAY 18

In the town   a bookshop   rooms lead to rooms   books
line the walls   she runs her fingers along their spines
    on a table of used books   finds
    a guidebook to the city   a century old

In one room   a spiral staircase   in another   a wall of glass
through a door   a courtyard
    on the far wall   a film plays
    air fills with the song of humpback whales

Fathom

some things we do are not innate   they're learned   they
tell us who we're connected to   where we belong   we call these
things   culture
  the oldest cultures are not human   they're from the ocean
  for generations researchers thought whales were solitary   40
million years ago   before we walked upright   before we sparked
fire   their brains exploded with complexity   consciousness
regions related to self and community grew   more elaborate
than any other brain   including ours   senses of sight and
sound merged   allowing whales to see one another   through
sound
  whales evolved   to build relationships   in the dark

air   liquid with blue light
whales glide   fins outspread

under water   sounds can take half an hour   to bend round
the horizon   or fade   in a matter of seconds and feet   sounds
constantly arrive   from different places   and times   somehow
humpbacks decipher an acoustic world   where past and present
arrive   all at once
  it's like knowing how each of the stars fit within time
  with just your ears

the film ends   she surfaces
voices resume

I felt so comfortable
when I started working with sound
because it was the way
I wanted to work with memory,
it was the way I wanted to
work with narrative. And
it was the way I wanted to
work with the audience.

When I heard Thomas Tallis'
choral, 'Spem in Alium',
I immediately saw it as
a sculptural piece. It
had 40 different harmonies.
I saw the score, and how
it moved, page after page
it would move, like this, like water
in a river moving around.

The soundwaves hitting your body
from 40 different speakers
effect you emotionally.
The sound goes totally into you.
And if it's the right space, it
reverberates within your body.

I love the feeling of a song
before you understand it,
when we're all playing deep inside
the moment, the song feels wild,
unbroken.

Soon we'll drag it into something
familiar, compliant, and
we'll put it in the stable with
all the other songs. But there's
a moment when the song is still
in charge and you're clinging on
for dear life.

One of my biggest pleasures
is to read a book,
fall in love with it
and never want to finish it.

Translating gives me the chance
to live through it again –
to get inside it
and be part of it.

Am I disturbing?

He pulls out a chair
a leaf flutters from a tree.

There is an exhibition of dolls.

Idol, doll

(a short talk)

Dolls have been made from so many things:
porcelain, leather, clay, bones,
ducks' bills, moss, rag, tin,
seed-pods, breadcrumbs, cardboard, cones,
withered fruit, wax, wool, paper,
birch bark, grass and gingerbread.
They have been stuffed with straw, feathers,
sawdust, bran, horsehair, cork, and wood.
Sometimes live birds
were enclosed in the hollow bodies of dolls.
Their frantic efforts to free themselves
gave the doll the appearance of being alive
or driven by clockwork
which amused children and adults alike.

Guided tour:

(This doll celebrates the notion that woman is a little world,
a perfectly proportioned universe)

The smallest doll in the world has
a black dot for each eye
a red dot for the nose and
a dark pink for rosy cheeks.
Hair is suggested by black paint.

Smaller than a 5 pence coin
this doll can sit and has
a hopping gait
due to the jointing system
locking arms and legs together.

The lower part of her
legs are painted white
to represent socks and
her feet are painted red
to suggest shoes.

Her upper arms and legs
are unpainted;
she was once dressed
though her clothes
have been lost.

Paper, person, doll
(a lecture)

The nature of paper
is as complicated
as that of a person.

It has many aspects
such as its strength when wet,
how to keep its shape etc.

Sustained effort is needed
to understand the complex qualities
of paper or a person just by looking.

Just as a person's chest hurts
when it is forcibly twisted, paper is strained
when folded against the grain.

　　　　She drifts off

...Basic point 4:
No matter how beautiful a person is
that beauty is cut in half by messy hair.
Dolls are the same.

The bodies of dolls

Before 1960 many male dolls
were originally female
with a standard doll's body
of narrow waist, and wide hips
– masculine identity signified
by hair and clothing.
This is a female doll dressed as a man
– notice the luxuriant black whiskers,
moustache and rosy lips.

Beautiful boy

Charles Pierotti made this doll
in the image of his only child
who died when still very young.
The fragile beauty of the infant is evoked
in the subtle pink colouring
of the wax, the large pale blue
glass eyes and the gold-blond mohair
curled over the forehead
and around the sides of the face.

The poet Rilke, on dolls

(a short film)

The doll was the first to make us aware
of that silence larger than life
which later breathed on us
again and again
whenever we came to the border of our existence.

    Are we not strange creatures,
    letting ourselves be guided
    to direct our earliest inclinations
    to where there is no hope
    of response?

A poet could fall under the domination of a marionette,
because the marionette has only imagination.
The doll has none,
and is exactly that much less a thing
as the marionette is more...
But this, in all its inevitability,
contains the secret of the doll's predominance.
Of you, doll-soul, one could never quite say where you really were,
whether you were at that moment in us
or in that drowsy creature
to whom we were constantly assigning you.

In the square   they buy grilled corn from a vendor
  elote with chilli and cheese
They part ways
  she turns back to look at his newly familiar form

At the corner shop   she chooses
avocado   tomato   onion   cucumber   lime
hears   from inside   whistles   answering whistles
Yesika emerges
    I was whistling to my cousin 2 streets over
    in Mazateco   our first language
    different tones change meaning
    We learned from our elders   who learned
    from the birds
        the whistle carries   further than we can see
        it's who we are
        who we have always been.

Home   she opens the guidebook

A good military band plays in the plaza   certain evenings
Sunday mornings   cloister-like portales   shaded walks of the
parks   then brilliant and animated   Saturday   market day
of the Indians of the neighbourhood   the visitor may obtain
the best views of native life   Mixtec and Zapotec Indians
one sees   usually undersized   considerable goitre among the
women

The more one sees   Mixtec and Zapotec tribes   stronger
grows the conviction their forebears were   in some way
linked with the Mongols   To the eyes of some   there is a
suspicious slant   certain facial characteristics   vaguely recall
the Cantonese and Fokienese   tonal quality of their speech
not unlike that of certain sections of Southern China   Some
of their women   every whit as unattractive as the Chinese
women of Canton and Amoy   the same excoriating voices
and vituperative speech.

She turns to the dictionary

colonise: *v.*

establish a colony

establish control over (the indigenous people of a colony)

appropriate (a place or domain) for one's own use

colony: *n.*

a country or area under the political control of another country and occupied by settlers from that country

settler: *n.*

a person who settles in an area, especially one with no or few previous inhabitants

settlement: *n.*

a place where people establish a community

an arrangement whereby property passes to a person or succession of people as dictated by the settlor

Morning   gap in the hedge
    what to do with this   belly-deep knowing
she hesitates   jumps
and like a flag   she is
all breath   bolting through water

Turning around she swims into the sun
below her   water light glimmers on the pool floor
like electricity   life force
like the collective soul   of something   of everything

Dwarf coatimundi

fair nomad
odd adroit cat

    fawn coat torn
    radiant wound

            unfair   I mourn
            an inward mantra

wait   a diamond curtain
a drift   into coda

Waking in the night
she tries to remember her brother's voice
the quiet of it

A girl brushes her hair in a nightdress of white and blue –
window open wide, she sleeps, eyes full of the night in blue.

On a rooftop, a boy, skinny, hair in his eyes, unwinds a spool,
lets fly with its glittering tail, his kite into the blue.

She wants cherries dark as blood, honeyed promise from the sun –
no blueberries, no plums – she has no appetite for blue.

With my tiny pen as skinny as a butterfly's hind legs
I persevere, with the ocean's tears I write in blue.

Beloved, your name is a prayer, a honeybee charm,
your voice in my ear, a meteorite out of the blue.

Long-eared owl

regal loner
legend
near-god

    adorn wood   wall

learned wanderer
gold-green-dweller

    allow wonder   awe

DAY 23

Walking to the bookshelf café
street after street leads to mountains   sky

In the courtyard   an old man folds brown paper
sharp folds and soft folds

   she remembers   after the Sewol ferry disaster
   people folded 1,000 white paper cranes
   for each child who perished

He sees her looking   calls her over

Creation requires time.
It took me 23 years
to develop this cicada

from initial inspiration
to the full development of folds.
Every creation emerges

from a series of variations
around the same theme, until it
expresses its own clearly
perceptible character.

Everywhere   people are making
a woman projects shadows on the far wall

For me, shadows symbolise
another dimension of
life – perhaps something even
more real than its holder.

In a shadow there is
little information
for the viewer – it is
basically a void.

Everything rests on
the right light – one will
make double shadows,
another, very
crisp shadows or
blurry ones.

Do the shadows we cast say something about us –
the distorted angling
of the sun behind us?

The more you fail, the more
you succeed. When everything is lost and you go on –
suddenly you have the feeling – illusion or not –
something new has opened up.

The form is always the measure of the obsession.

In this chaos that we live in
I like to put some order.
I like straight lines. I like angles.

If you're going to be basic
you can never fail. I have a
painting I think is finished –
I take something out – it's better.

    It's not easy but I like it
    and if I didn't have this
    I would just sit waiting for God.

There is a saying: 'If you wait
for the bus, the bus will come.'
I wait almost a century
for the bus – and it came.

Keel-billed toucan

notable local
   black-cloaked
   lake-blue ankle   toe

tonal beak   a delicate elation
   a candle-lit bell

lulled talk
      an inaudible knell

DAY 26

Radio on   blanket round her
a woman speaks

> *In the arms of your voice*
> *...with lips, half-earth, half-night,*
> *a heart of dust, and another of wind*

> *I'm speaking of this love*
> *navigating through fog,*
> *this love, this love.*

she slips in and out of sleep

> *I find you sometimes, in a face you never had,*
> *in impermanence you didn't deserve.*
> *And silence lifts its head to look at me.*

> *Now we return at night,*
> *trees hold on to their birds*
> *and tiredness extends its tongue to sing in our ears.*

Deer mouse

o mouse
demure doe

      rouse   red suede drum
      resume

DAY 28

Morning   cloud
under water   blue tiles lie flatly

   a leaf hangs
   barely there   rise and fall

                                 sudden sun

below   her shadow appears   swims before her

     the glimmer   unexpected comes

Nine-banded armadillo

dear old one
mild armored animal
   medallioned
   droll eared

adored elder
   millennia borne
   iron demeanour abandoned

        dreamland   a liminal realm
       a lonelier ballad

DAY 31

Night   stars   ~~crickets~~   grasshoppers   a dog
barks   answering barks across the valley

voices from the house next door

a moth taps against the window
mistaking lamplight for the moon
Soon there are more moths more insects tapping the glass

She left us so quickly, so surprisingly...
I believe that in the end she left
everything behind and felt free.

So I want to offer her this moment
of lightness, this feeling
of weightlessness.

I still haven't dreamed about you.
I get news of you from Daphnis who dreams
of you all the time.
But it's not the same.

She picks up her brother's book

If you want something too much
it won't come

Tries to let go of wanting.

Elegy

For a boy of 8 or 10
the worm can be
a great teacher, especially

a strong, healthy creature
kept in damp moss
to clean and harden his skin.

Such a worm,
hard, bright
and brilliantly red

should be fished
on a No. 10 or 8 offset hook
or even a 6.

Any limber pole
with a length of line from the tip
will do

but an old, soft fly rod
with a simple reel
and 10-pound monofilament is best.

So equipped, a boy can go
to any trout water in spring and early summer
when the water is high

cast his worm in
and let the current carry it to
the likely spots.

Some places are good for big fish
some for small fish
and some are a waste of time.

There is a difference between the feel
of the lake or river bed
and the feel of a fish mouthing the worm.

There is a way of raising the rod tip firmly to strike
the hook into the fish
without breaking the leader.

There is a right moment for this
and a wrong moment.
One must be quicker with a little fish than a big one.

The testing time and the real learning time
is in summer and fall
when the water is low and clear.

Best now to work upstream
approaching the fish from behind
keeping the head low and the rod low

stalking the fish
rather than searching,
sneaking up on the likely places.

The cast is a delicate sidearm swing that slides
the worm forward
through the air (drawing a few coils of loose line

from the left hand)
and plops it in at the head of the run.
It comes drifting back.

The line is slowly and carefully recovered
through the rings of the rod
keeping pace but never pulling on the worm.

Suddenly the line stops
holds against the current
and the fish is there.

The time will come
when the boy is ready to fish a fly
and the worm has little more to teach him.

Mountain lakes or lowland lakes,
rushing streams
or quiet meadow streams,

tidal estuaries
or salt-water shallows,
all have their charms and moods.

Spring, summer and fall,
the fly-fisherman moves quietly through them,
disturbing little, seeing much.

How it begins

A man and a woman press close as flowers
press to the pages of a book   her pale foot slips
from its sandal in the vaulted space of a kiss
and the way his hands hold her face
is the way leaves hold a bud before it flowers

Now this
A woman alone in a crowd watches
a strong brown river struggle to hold
the whale that swam down the city's glittering throat
        and the air presses
        heavy as grief against her enormous softness

And if a woman and a boy stand before a glass coffin that holds
the bones of a northern bottlenose whale
the softness of his hand will be enormous
as she tells him how a story that began with a kiss
        despite the enormous hole at its heart   can hold a boy
and a river that began with rainwater or snowmelt
        can briefly hold a whale before letting it go
                to spill from its mouth into the ocean
                stories of whales and boys and all it has known

NOTES

The taxidermy poems employ an anagram form inspired by the French post-surrealist group OULIPO (Ouvroir de Littérature Potentielle), a gathering of mathmeticians, scientists and writers who embrace constraint as a means of triggering ideas and inspiration.

'Fathom' draws on the words of Dr Ellen Garland and Dr Michelle Fournet in the film of the same name.

'Idol, Doll', 'Guided Tour', 'The Bodies of Dolls', 'Beautiful Boy' and 'Paper, Person, Doll' use found text from multiple sources.

'The Poet, Rilke, on Dolls' quotes from Rainer Maria Rilke's essay 'On the wax dolls of Lotte Pritzel'.

The guidebook refers to *Terry's Guide to Mexico* (The Riverside Press, 1909) from which I have quoted

'In the arms of your voice' is an extract from the poem 'En el árbol de la voz' by Susana Chavez Castillo, translated from the Spanish by me.

'Elegy' employs text from *A Primer of Fly-Fishing* by Roderick Haig-Brown, and I have also cited extracts on tying flies.

I am grateful to the artists whose work and thinking has inspired and resonated with me; their words generated the following poems:

'We made our own brushes'
'There was a strict discipline'   Imran Qureshi

'Ultimately, as an artist'   Kwame Kwei-Armah

'For me the artistic enterprise is'   Meena Kandasamy

'Art is born of necessity.'   August Wilson
'When we apply paint'
'When we apply gold leaf'

'They are always asking me'   Imran Qureshi

'At Francis Bacon at the Tate'   Jack Vettriano

'You do ask yourself'   Don McCullin

'I never write *about*'   Adania Shibli

'Many sufferings stem'   Samira Makhmalbaf

'New in the company I didn't yet grasp' Anna Wehsarg

'I saw her do Café Müller so often'   Helena Pikon

'She was so beautiful to watch'   Julie Shanahan

'I felt so comfortable when I started'   Janet Cardiff

'I love the feeling of a song'   Nick Cave

'One of my biggest pleasures'   Lucila Cordone

'Creation requires time'   Akira Yoshizawa

'For me shadows symbolise'   Kumi Yamashita
'Do the shadows we cast say something
about us'   Alberto Giacometti

'In this chaos that we live in'   Carmen Herrera

'She left us so quickly, so surprisingly...' Regina Advento

'I still haven't dreamed about you.'   Clémentine Deluy

ACKNOWLEDGEMENTS:

The work and ideas of taxidermy artists Divya Anantharaman and Polly Morgan were key sources of inspiration.

Grateful acknowledgements to *The Hudson Review* and *New England Review* where the white mouse poems and 'Elegy' first appeared.

Thanks to Syima Aslam at Bradford Literature Festival for commissioning the poem that became 'How It Begins'; and to Elhum Shakerifar at Poetry in Motion: the festival of Contemporary Iranian Cinema, for commissioning the poem that became 'Ghazal with Rain and Birds'. Thanks also to the Royal Society of Literature for a Brookleaze Grant to research poems on dolls and dollmakers.

Heartfelt thanks to my editor and publisher, Neil Astley, for his encouragement and guidance; to my students for accompanying me in thinking and questioning; and to my family for the house of love, with its corners and comforts, that makes this writing life possible.